THE SIGNIFICANCE OF MAKING UP YOUR BED

Pastor Alfred A. Dingle Sr.

Diligence Publishing Company
Bloomfield, New Jersey

The Scripture in this book is from various versions of the Bible.

THE SIGNIFICANCE OF MAKING UP YOUR BED

Copyright © 2018 Alfred A. Dingle Sr.
c/o Diligence Publishing Company
P.O. Box 2476
Bloomfield, New Jersey

All Rights Reserved

No part of this book may be reproduced in any form without the written permission from the author except for brief passages included in a review.

To contact Rev. Alfred A. Dingle Sr. to preach or speak at your church, organization, seminar or conference email: revaldingle@yahoo.com or contact Alfred Dingle on Facebook

THE SIGNIFICANCE OF MAKING UP YOUR BED

ISBN: 978-0-9963833-9-4

Printed in the United States

Index

Dedication, Special Thanks and Preface

Chapter One
Introduction to Making up Your Bed............13

Chapter Two
The Instructions of Making Up Your Bed....17

Chapter Three
The Function of the Bed...............................23

Chapter Four
The Meaning of Making Your Bed.................33

Chapter Five
What is Required
Prior to Making Your Bed............................37

Chapter Six
The Lessons in Making up Your Bed............43

Chapter Seven
Making Up Your Final Bed...........................55

About the Author

DEDICATION

To my loving wife, Vanessa Dingle;

To my Pastor and Dad, Pastor Simon Dingle and Mom, Rev. Laverne Dingle;

To the Memorial Baptist Church in Newark, NJ;

To Apostle Paula Ford and the Greater Mt. Sinai Church of God Unity Pentecostal Family;

To all my children, by birth, by marriage and by divine appointment;

To all my family;

To Dr. Albert J. Lewis and WGMA;

To the group, 4 for Christ;

To the Crossroads of Life Christian Bookstore.

SPECIAL THANKS

To God be the Glory for the things He has done. I give thanks to my heavenly Father and my Lord and Savior Jesus the Christ. The Almighty God has allowed me once again to share what He has given me. I am in awe of Thee oh God. When I think of His grace and mercy, I can't help but say thank You Lord. I never thought I would ever be an author, but God. I could not do this without Him.

I thank my beautiful wife Vanessa, for her love, patience and input in my writing ministry and overall ministry. She gives me the balance I need. Thanks for having my back. Thank you, my love, and thank God for you.

I thank my Dad and my Mom, Pastor Simon and Rev. Laverne Dingle of the Central Baptist Church in Bayonne, New Jersey for your love and support down through the years. Thanks for all your words of encouragement.

Thanks to all my children and grandchildren by birth and by divine connection who showed me that love is thicker than blood. Thank you for your great love and care you all show unto me. Deacon Alfred A. and Deaconess Natasha Dingle; Clarysha Dingle; Christopher Dingle; Minister Sharlene Jackson; Youth Pastor Steven and Dominique Flagg; Kim Phillips-Benton; Tiffini Hill; Luis J.R. Jackson; Maquia Liptrot; and all my grandchildren. Thank you for your respect.

To all my family: my brother, Minister Simon Jr., sisters, Laura Ethel, Van Dora, Patricia, Sandra, Rosa, and Janice, in-laws, aunts, uncles, cousins, etc., thank you.

Thanks to Crossroads of Life Christian Bookstore for supporting and encouraging me as an author, Pastor and an artist.

I thank Dr. Albert J. Lewis for his support as well.

To the members of the Memorial Baptist Church, thanks for the chance to minister to you all down through the years. Thanks to my publisher, Pastor Rebecca Simmons and Diligence Publishing Company for the awesome job done and for all your encouragement. God bless you and your husband, Pastor Anthony Simmons.

In Loving Memory

In memory of my dear departed mother Vera L. Dingle. Hopefully, I'm making you proud. I will never stop missing you. My late grandparents, Pastor Shephard and Evangelist Laura Dingle. Prayerfully, I'm living up to your vision of ministry. Bishop Clyde and Mother Harris, Pastor Milton "Pop" Byrd and all other departed loved ones. You all are missed greatly.

In memory of all my departed family that had a great influence in my life, both Davenport and Dingle, such as: My grandparents, the late Rev. Shephard and Evangelist Laura Dingle, who saw my calling at my young age and prayed my strength, offering guidance to me to do the work of the Lord. To all who are too numerous to mention, I thank God for you.

PREFACE

Writing this book has altered my view of making up my bed. It has given me a different outlook as well as a different insight on what it means to make up your bed. I can no longer observe this task as I once did. Every time I make up my bed, these concepts and the lessons that God has given me to share comes to mind of the significance of making my bed. They motivate me to do more and to strive to use these precepts to their fulness. The effect the contents of this book had on me, I pray that it will have similar or greater impact on the readers.

CHAPTER 1

Introduction to Making Up Your Bed

From the dawn of mankind's need for sleep, there existed the need for a place to sleep. Although places and what was slept on has evolved, the need for sleep has not. Beds and their designs continue to evolve, but sleep and the need thereof will remain constant in time.

This concept of making up your bed is not original in its act, but I hope my presentation of it is unique. It's not original because it's something that we were taught when we were young. People in the military or familiar with its operation know the criteria involved with bed making. So, this is not original in its thought; But the presentation of this precept I will give it to you as it was given to me. Once again, although the job isn't new, it is my task to take that which was taught and state it in a unique fashion. In ministry, we call this method, "contemporizing," which is basically taking old statements, teachings and concepts, translating them into modern day language, statements, teachings and concepts and explaining how they're relevant in today's times. In other words, saying something old in a new way.

In my search for information to write on this topic, I came across a video of a graduation Commencement Address at the University of Texas in Austin in 2014 given by Admiral William H. McRaven. He used this precept for a brief portion of his speech. William Harry McRaven, according to Wikipedia, is a retired United States Navy admiral who last served as the ninth commander of the United States Special Operations Command from August 8, 2011 to August 28, 2014. From 2015 to 2018, he was the chancellor of the University of Texas System.

This is a portion of that great address:

"If you wanna change the world, start off by making your bed. If you make your bed every morning, you will have accomplished your first task of the day. It will give you a small sense of pride, and will encourage you to do another task, and another, and another. And by the end of the day that one task completed will have turned into many tasks completed. Making your bed will reinforce the fact that the little things in life matter. If you can't do the little things right, you'll never be able to do the big things right. And if by chance, you have a miserable day, you will come home to a bed that is made; that you made. And a

THE SIGNIFICANCE OF MAKING UP YOUR BED

made bed gives you encouragement that tomorrow will be better."

CHAPTER 2

The Instructions for Making Up Your Bed

When I was growing up, at times I and my brother had to share the same room. My family was not privileged to have a big house where each of us could have our own room. Although I came 4th after my brother and 2 sisters, I'm sure that the sleeping arrangements in most families of humble beginnings had and continue to have similar patterns.

We didn't have a lot of fancy things, but we were greatly loved. When you are very young, siblings and or family share the same room and even the same bed. As the children grow, efforts are made to move to larger dwellings or other adjustments are made to give children a space of their own. That's what I did with my own children. We lived in a four-room apartment in which my, at that time, two children shared a room. But when my third child came along, we had to upgrade. By the grace of God and hard work, I was blessed to purchase a house. Now finally, I was able to provide each child with their own room. I had to move some walls, but it was done.

Although time and increase of the family brought about changes, one of the many things that remained the same was the lessons and instructions that were given to us at an early age. There was something that my mother, God rest her soul, expected from us. That was to make up our beds. Whether it was our own or the one shared, we had to make up the bed. In addition to making the bed, it had to be done to her satisfaction. I am now 55 years old at this time in 2018, and I am just coming to understand the true importance of that and many lessons taught to me by my parents.

It's funny how a simple task like making your bed can possess important lessons for life. What appeared to be chores given to us was actually valuable lessons to prepare us for the future and independence. Because, we as children in most part did not want to do chores, we on many occasions missed the lessons being taught to us. So many times, it had to be repeated to us things like cleaning up your room, sweeping and mopping the floor, taking out the trash, picking up after yourself, etc. But in my opinion, I think the last thing we consider gaining messages from is making up your bed. I believe that it's safe to say that a few of the jobs we were told to do growing up were not considered by our parents or guardians to hold deep, intellectual concepts.

Much of what we were instructed to do, they too received many of the same instructions by their parents or guardians. Parents tend to parent as they were parented. Many parents who express love and support to their children do so because that's what they received. Likewise, some parents that are abusers do so because some of them were abused. Some raise their children in the church because they were raised in the church and recognized the benefit of the church setting. Some speak using profanity, hurtful and insulting words because that's what they received.

Parents and guardians hand down what was handed down to them. Lest I be misunderstood or be wrongfully accused of making it sound like once a cycle or style of parenting begins, it will always be the same, let me suggest this perspective.

People do change methods of child raising. Some people overcome abuse and neglect and go on to become wonderful loving parents or guardians. And to the contrary, some can drop the ball. There are several conditions which can cause a deviation or an alteration in parenting styles and produce differences in reference to parenting.

1. If the parents or guardian didn't care for some of the things and conditions under which they were raised, they will do something different.
2. If the parents or guardians believed that there was something additional they could have used growing up.
3. A combining of parental styles of two different parenting styles.
4. Some parents or guardians recognize that some children need different teachings.

Although we can spend more time in this area of discussion, we will not for the purpose of focusing on the main point of this book.

I know I didn't think about this at all before, but one day as I got up to go about my day, the Spirit of God zoomed my attention on this task of making up my bed. It was in the year of 2018 when the Holy Spirit brought this to my attention. He let me know that there was a significance and some lessons to be abstracted from this act of tidiness. Making your bed can help you to compartmentalize your life when one understands its importance.

CHAPTER 3

The Function of The Bed

Let me begin this chapter by stating that the bed is designed to be a temporary dwelling place and not a permanent position. Even though the bed isn't the only means by which people can obtain what they can get from a bed, there's nothing that can replace a nice, comfortable bed. If you allow your bed to become a permanent place, its occupier then is facing a great problem.

The bed has numerous functions and uses.

1. Rest

2. Relaxation

3. Recovery and restoration

4. Relationship

5. Earthly departure

Rest:

The first function we want to emphasize is rest. The one who occupies the bed uses it to get rested. As we go through the daily tasks required for us to live in this life, we can and will get tired, worn out and fatigued. At the end of our day or at the end of our tasks, our bodies require rest that it may be reenergized for the next day. The body needs to get rest to go about the next task. The bed is there to help us to get comfortable and to get sleep that we may be able to function. It has been scientifically proven that the body requires at least 6-8 hours of quality sleep. There is a scripture in the book of Psalms that I've quoted to a few people about rest that was actually quoted back to me.

<u>Psalm 23:2 KJV</u>

"He maketh me to lie down in green pastures:"

We can get so busy and have so many plans, we can exhaust ourselves. If individuals try to operate without proper rest, it can lead to unhealthiness, mistakes, accidents, lack of focus, confusion, brain fog and other behaviors that can put someone and others in danger.

<u>Relaxation:</u>

The second use we will talk about is relaxation. The bed is a place where its occupier can relax and unwind. Sometimes the body does not need a full 6 to 8 hours of sleep at the moment, it just needs to get at ease. Laying in a nice comfortable bed can help you relax not only your body but also your mind and your spirit.

Recovery and Restoration:

The third use we want to bring attention to is recovery and restoration. The bed is used for recovery and restoration. In this life we can and do get sick. We all can and will fall ill from some type of germ or virus. From the common cold to something major, something will place us in a position which will cause the need for healing. The bed helps the body to lay in a position so the process of recovery and restoration of health may be gained.

Relationship:

Fourthly, the bed is also a place where intimacy and sharing in relationship with your mate takes place. The time that the bed can become a place of activity is when couples express love in a physical fashion. It becomes a place of activity when a loving couple shares love through sexual activity. Husbands and wives share intimate moments in bed both physically and emotionally. A couple can gain a deeper connection when they participate in loving conversation. It is much easier to dialog with your mate when you are in a relaxed state. Couples can share their thoughts with each other about the future, their hopes and dreams, and what is hoped to be accomplished. In my opinion, even expressing the love you feel for others verbally seems to be more special. You get to know each other in greater emotional and intellectual ways. There is a development of oneness in an emotional and intellectual way. Plus, there is something special about sharing intimate physical moments of love-making with the one you love. There is a development of oneness in a physical manner. This is what Adam says in the book of Genesis when God the Creator united him with woman.

Genesis 2:23 KJV

"And Adam said, This is now bone of my bones, and flesh of my flesh: she shall be called Woman, because she was taken out of Man.

24 Therefore shall a man leave his father and his mother and shall cleave unto his wife: and they shall be one flesh.

Therefore, it is extremely important that you be aware of who you get involved with emotionally, intellectually, spiritually and especially and specifically sexually.

1 Corinthians 6:16 KJV

Do you not know that he who unites himself with a prostitute is one with her in body? For it is said, "The two will become one flesh"

THE FUNCTION OF THE BED

Hebrews 13:4 KJV

"Marriage [is] honorable in all, and the bed undefiled: but whoremongers and adulterers God will judge."

When I lived in Jersey City, I recall being awakened by a young lady having a discussion with her mate. I'm not sure of all the details, because I only caught a piece of the conversation. I don't know if it was her husband or not. I can only assume. But I know for a certainty that the relationship was supposed to be one of commitment and monogamy. But for the sake of this point, we will consider him as her husband.

She made the heartbreaking discovery that he had been unfaithful to her. She expressed the hurt she felt by his cheating. But not only was she upset with his affair, but the affair took place in the bed they shared. She continued to repeat that he had done this in their bed. He had another woman in the bed that was supposed to be exclusively for them to share.

Earthly Departure:

The fifth and final use of the bed is death. Many people die in bed, that bed becomes their place of departure and transition out of this world. It is the most undesired use of a bed. But even those who leave this world that die in a different place, end up, in most part, in the same condition. The older generations would make statements that referred to their last moments of their lives as their dying bed. The coffin is made in the fashion of a bed. The coffin which contains the remains of a person is laid in a grave which is considered to be their final resting place. But there's a difference between a bed for sleep and a coffin. To echo a previous statement, the bed is designed to be a temporary dwelling place and

THE FUNCTION OF THE BED

not a permanent position. There's a difference between a bed and a coffin.

CHAPTER 4

The Meaning of Making Your Bed

It's one thing to straighten your bed and another thing to make up your bed. When one straightens their bed, it's just to reorganize the sheets and the blankets. Getting and sleeping in bed will cause the sheets and covers to become disorganized. A person's style of sleeping and how much a person moves in their sleep will determine how disorganized the linens and blankets will become. Some people do a lot of tossing and turning in an effort to achieve a comfortable sleeping position. This causes a bundling and tangling of the sheets and covers. Also, items get lost like socks, remotes, head scarves, underwear, food crumbs, etc. So, people have a tendency of straightening or reorganizing the bed so they can once again lay in it. But when one makes up their bed, they make up their bed with the intention not to return to it until a later time. It would be counterproductive to go through the process of making up your bed completely, only to jump back into it and return it back to disarray.

If it's going to be done properly, it requires tucking in the sheets, making sure that the sheets are smooth, placing the blankets in a neat and orderly fashion, fluffing the pillows and laying them in order and changing the linens if necessary. I've been told and obtained reference through TV programs and films, that in the military, the sheets must be so tight that you can bounce a quarter off the bed. If that could not be done, it wasn't made correctly and would have to be redone adequately. Some people even go as far as ironing the linens before they are put on the bed. I'm not talking about just merely running a hot iron over them but pressing them using starch. Some people like their beds to look picturesque as though you are seeing it in a showroom display. Making your bed halfway truly should only be done when you plan to get back in the bed immediately.

CHAPTER 5

What Is Required Prior To Making Your Bed?

There are two great moments that transpire prior to making your bed. These two events display the blessings a person is allowed to experience that is vitally necessary before a person can make up their bed. Those two are waking up and getting up.

Wake Up:

A great thing has been manifested in your day when you wake up. Because you can't do anything until you first wake up; Not just open your eyes but have an awareness that you are alive and a sense of who you are. In other words, being in your right mind. It may sound as though I am contradicting myself, but there are some people who only have their eyes open and are still asleep. They are not aware of what's going on around them or in the world. There are people who operate with their, to reference Bishop T D Jakes in one of his sermons, "Eyes Wide Shut." Then you have people who are ill, and some are hospitalized that don't know that they are here. It is a blessing when you can wake up and know that you are still alive. I often say that things may not be the way you want them to be, but they can always be worse. So, I've learned how to appreciate things being as well as they are at that moment. If you had an unpleasant yesterday and your morning isn't to your liking, remember, it can always be worse. But also remember that there's always a chance for better. As long as you have breath in you, and are aware of self, there's an opportunity to be blessed or to be a blessing. So, thank God for waking up.

Get Up:

The second great moment in life that displays the blessings of God is the ability to get up. Just because someone wakes up doesn't automatically translate to them getting up. Before you can make up your bed, you must first get out of the bed. It is impossible to make up your bed while you are still laying in it. Making up your bed is not an inside job. It can't be done from an inward position, it must be done from the outside. You must depart from it. It's a task that requires an external position.

Why Some Don't Get Up:

Some people unfortunately are bedridden and unable to get up. Disease or unfortunate circumstances can prevent a person from rising out of bed. It's a disappointing situation to be awake but unable to get out of bed. There are also those whose mental state of mind prohibits them from getting up. There are those who struggle with depression and are trapped in their sadness. The depressed state of emotion causes them to believe that there is no reason to get up.

There's another reason why some people wake up but don't get up. Some people are just lazy and want things done for them. The Bible has something to say about people like this.

<u>*Proverbs 20:13 KJV*</u>
"Love not sleep, lest thou come to poverty; open thine eyes, and thou shalt be satisfied with bread."

<u>*New International Version*</u>
"Do not love sleep or you will grow poor; stay awake and you will have food to spare."

If the Lord God has blessed you with the strength to get up, then get up and do what you can do while you can do it.

The Need to Get Up:

Getting up is needed to get moving. I recollect the time when people were instructed after an operation and medical procedure to stay in bed. But now, doctors instruct people who can to get out of bed and walk around as soon as possible. Medical studies have shown that mobility promotes healing and gets the blood circulating. Because I'm not a doctor, I can't speak about all the medical benefits of getting out of bed. But I do know this. Laying in the bed can increase the possibility of pneumonia and muscle decline and can cause the development of bed sores.

So, I repeat, if the Lord God has blessed you with the strength to get up, then get up and do what you can do while you can do it.

CHAPTER 6

The Lessons in Making Up Your Bed

As we contemplate on this task of making up your bed, the lessons that we can abstract from this are the following:

1. One of the things the Lord brought to my attention was that making your bed signifies your recognition that the time for sleep is over for now. Making up your bed demonstrates that you are cognizant of the fact that sleep is a temporary act of inactivity. Sleep is compartmentalizing a moment in time and the bed, in most part,

other than people participating in intimate activity, is a place of temporary inactivity. AKA, sleeping. As was mentioned in a previous chapter, how it would be counterproductive to go through the process of making up your bed completely, only to jump back into it. Especially if it was made correctly and neatly. Making the bed reveals that you are preparing to move forward in the day. It is making the statement that the realization that what I am responsible for doing won't get done if I don't get on the move.

Proverbs 19:15 KJV
"Laziness brings on deep sleep, and an idle soul will suffer hunger."

Proverbs 28:19 KJV
"The one who works his land will have

plenty of food, but whoever chases fantasies will have his fill of poverty."

So therefore, it is extremely vital that a person understand that in order to achieve something you must do something. Making up your bed can be an excellent reminder of one's responsibility.

2. Next, making your bed will be your first task of the day that you complete in which you will be aware of. Although very few, if any, may see it done, it will affect you. Simply because it can be viewed as unfinished business. People can observe your appearance. People can be aware of your personal hygiene; Good bad or indifferent. But the only person other than yourself that will see your bed made up is the one whom with you share it. Besides that, it's the people who you allow in your

bedroom. Once again, I quote Admiral William H. McRaven from his graduation Commencement Address at the University of Texas in Austin in 2014. *"If you wanna change the world, start off by making your bed. If you make your bed every morning, you will have accomplished your first task of the day. It will give you a small sense of pride, and will encourage you to do another task, then another, and another."*

3. Another lesson is this. Making your bed displays the blessing that you have the use and activities of your body as well as having control of your extremities. It is worth repeating that waking up doesn't automatically translate to getting up. In the same way, getting up doesn't automatically translate to having the use and activities of one's body, let alone control of one's faculties. There are many people who may

be able to get out of bed but are limited in the functions of their body. People have disabilities in body and mind which prevents them from being in control. When you can make up your bed yourself, it is a blessing.

4. Because you have the use and control of your body, making up your bed gives the opportunity to move your body. It can be viewed as one of your first physical activities of the day. I have learned that in the morning when you wake up from sleeping, it's good to stretch and move your limbs to get ready for other activities. It may not have been considered before but making up your bed involves lifting your arms and moving your legs and other parts of the body. Making your bed can assist you in getting on the move. It's like having your first moderate exercise of the day.

5. In addition, making up your bed shows that you are aware of time. If you are planning on doing something and going somewhere, then you must give yourself enough time. In order to make up your bed, you must get up early enough to do so before you start your day. If the events of your day involve time restraints and arrival times, then it's necessary to have sufficient time to make your bed and do other things before going forth.

6. Making up your bed also shows that you care about how and where you sleep. I would be very displeased if my wife and I went to a hotel and went into the room only to observe the room being unclean and the bed unmade. There would be an instant request for a change of venue. I would expect a refund if any money had been prepaid and go to a different hotel. I recall

the time when my wife Vanessa and I went on a two night get away. We didn't go out of state, we just went to another city. I booked the hotel online and looked at pictures of the facility. The hotel seemed to be decent in its appearance and its price, so I booked it. Unfortunately, the pictures didn't show us the true condition of the hotel. When we arrived at the room, we saw the carpet didn't have the greatest appearance and the room was quite beneath our usual standard. But worse of all was the condition of the bed. Not only did the covers have large burns in them but stains on the liner. It was disgusting. It disturbed us because we care about how and where we sleep. Fortunately, the weekend turned in our favor because as we left that disappointing situation, right next to it was a hotel just recently constructed that we checked into. Our displeasure of the previous hotel was greatly overshadowed by the splendor of the change in hotels. Although we will never forget that unpleasant experience, we likewise will never forget the neat and clean hotel in which we were well pleased.

7. Making your bed can not only change the appearance of your bedroom, but it can also change the mood. You can clean the bedroom, but it still has the appearance of untidiness because the bed is unmade. I believe it for the fact that the bed is primarily the largest object in the room and is the focal point of the room. That's why it's called the "bedroom." When you are worn out or just want to relax, it's soothing coming to your bedroom and seeing a nice, organized bed. As we alluded to in the chapter, "The Function of the Bed," the bed

is a wonderful place for a husband and wife to share time with each other and express love with one another in a physical manner. What assists in setting the mood for lovemaking is a well-prepared bed. Creating a romantic setting in the bedroom, especially for women, is a loving and caring gesture of expression prior to physical participation.

8. Making your bed helps you see that every task has value and purpose. One may ask, how can making up your bed make you aware that every task has value and purpose? Hold in consideration that the only one that will see your bed other than you is the person who you share your bed with if any. Other than that, are the other people who you allow to enter into your bedroom. That one undone task means that you left something undone. It may not seem

like much to you to leave your bed unmade, but it does matter. The reason why is because of the next lesson we can learn from making up our bed.

9. Making your bed prepares you for the end of your day and rest at the end of your task. For those of us who have jobs and other responsibilities, we will get tired from the fulfillment of those responsibilities. When you've had an exhausting and hectic day, the last thing you need is to have to organize your bed. It's always better and more efficient to just be able to pull back the covers and get into bed. I remember someone giving me advice about moving. He said whenever you are moving, the first thing to move is your bed. Take it and set it up before you complete moving. Because when you finish moving, you have a bed ready for you to lay down in and sleep.

Having your place ready for rest and relaxation set up in advance is a great way to end your day.

10. Making up your bed exemplifies the fact that you have a bed to sleep in. Quite often people who have a bed take for granted the bed we were blessed to sleep in. Some people are in an unfortunate situation to where they have no bed in which to sleep, Or the bed that they sleep in is not their own. I've witnessed people sleeping on benches, and on the ground. I've heard of people who slept where ever they found a place to lay their heads. It is a blessing when you have a bed that you can call your own to sleep in. In addition to that, the bed that some people lay in isn't theirs to claim. Some people have to sleep or have slept in shelters and the bed in which they slept was only used by them if it was available. It

THE SIGNIFICANCE OF MAKING UP YOUR BED

is a blessing when you can lay down in a bed that you can say, it's mine. Be grateful that you have a bed that you can make up.

CHAPTER 7

Making Up Your Last Bed

The Final Chapter

This bed is unlike a regular bed and may very well be the most important bed you will ever make up. Making up what will be your final bed is different than making up a regular bed. Simply because making up a regular bed is something you do bodily. Making up beds that we sleep in bodily is in the tangible and physical. But this bed in which I refer to in this last chapter is in the spiritual and the eternal. Unlike the tangible bed upon which the physical body can lie, this bed is invisible to the naked eye. All people may not have a tangible bed, but all have a spiritual bed. Your actual physical bed may be larger or smaller, fancier or less fancy, prettier or uglier, neater or dirtier than others, but it won't matter at the end. But just like it is a good thing to prepare your natural bed for sleep, it is of the utmost importance that you prepare yourself for your last breath. In other words, where will you spend eternity?

As I forestated in the previous chapters that the bed is used for many things, one of them is rest. My point is simple. The concept that I am referring to is preparing your soul for its final resting place. We all need to be prepared to die. Death is inevitable, and we are all subject to it. There are different beliefs about life after death and some don't believe it at all; but because I am a believer in God's Word, I am persuaded that there is life after this present existence. The question is, where are you going to spend "Eternity?" Where will you set up and make up your bed for rest from the toils of this world? Although you can avoid making up your physical bed, this one you cannot avoid. Whether you believe it or not, there is a bed that has been set up for us all. We all will come to the point of death. We all have a dying bed.

<u>Hebrews 9:27 KJV</u>
"And as it is appointed unto men once to die, but after this the judgement:"

We all have a dying bed. We all will leave this world one day. What I mean by making up your dying bed is preparing yourself to stand before God the Almighty. Where is your resting place going to be located? It's not a plot here on earth, but that place in the hereafter. Every person that was, is being and will be born, was born with a predetermined destination. According to the scriptures, that place is eternal damnation.

Because of the sin of Adam, we became subject to the consequence of that sin. We were all born in sin and shaped in iniquity. But because of Jesus' life, His death, His burial and His resurrection, all have an opportunity to relocate where their final resting place will be.

I'm not saying to constantly live your life focused on dying, but live knowing that when the time comes to lay on your dying bed, you will be at peace. Live life knowing that you have a place prepared for you. All that receive Jesus the Christ, THE WORD MADE FLESH, will have a location for that spiritual bed. Jesus said in

Matthew 14:1-3 KJV

1. *Let not your heart be troubled: ye believe in God, believe also in me.*
2. *In my Father's house are many mansions: if it were not so, I would have told you. I go to prepare a place for you.*

3. *And if I go and prepare a place for you, I will come again, and receive you unto myself; that where I am, there ye may be also.*

But I must also inform all the readers of this book that this bed, if you want to spend eternity with God the Father and our Lord and Savior Jesus the Christ, can't be made just any kind of way. This bed can't be made with hatred in your heart, it must be made with love.

This bed can't be made with envy and strife, but with compassion and mercy. If you attempt to make this dying bed with the wrong attitude and perceptions, the location of it will remain the same and your eternal destination will not change.

Similar to our natural bed, we only lie in it temporarily but eventually, we will rise from it. This dying bed is only to transport us into eternity. When we are awakened, where will we be when we arise? Will it be Heaven or Hell? Will we wake up to everlasting peace or never-ending torment? Will you be with the Lord or with Satan and his demons in eternal damnation? This is why the older generation used to say "Lord, make up my dying bed."

How do you make this bed? It has no sheets nor pillowcases. This bed has no mattress or box spring. This bed has no bed frame or head board. How do we make up this bed? It first begins with acknowledging that you are a sinner and repenting of your sins. You must accept Jesus as Savior and Lord through which we have our sins forgiven and we are in right standing with God the Father. We make up this bed through praise, worship, prayer and aspiring to live a holy life in God. We make up this bed through the study of God's Word. We make up this bed when we strive to apply God's Word to our lives. Although there are no tangible items used in the making of this bed, there is a Comforter. Not a tangible, physical comforter, but a spiritual one. An actual comforter is what we put on our beds not only to beautify our beds and the appearance of the room, but it's primary use is to cover us and keep us warm. Our spiritual Comforter is the Holy Spirit. He beautifies us, covers us and keeps us warm.

When we are wrapped in the comfort of God's love, we feel safe and secure. We have a peace that passes all understanding. Hallelujah!!!!

St. John 14:16 KJV
And I will pray the Father, and he shall give you another Comforter, that he may abide with you forever;

My parents taught my siblings and I a bedtime prayer to pray before we went to sleep when we were very young. We were taught to go on our knees and say, "Now I lay me down to sleep, I pray *the Lord, my soul to keep. If I should die before I wake, I pray the Lord, my soul to take."*

This little childhood prayer I taught to my children. and I pray that they teach it to theirs and so on. This little childhood prayer was our thoughtful, loving parents' way of teaching and preparing us for death if it were to come unexpectedly. Even though this was a bedtime prayer, this mentality should be adhered to every moment of our lives. For, you never know when your life will expire. But in the event that you have time before your demise, and while yet in your right mind, it is good to ask the Lord to receive you.

<u>*Luke 23:46 KJV*</u>
"And when Jesus had cried with a loud voice, he said, 'Father, into thy hands I commend my spirit:' and having said thus, he gave up the ghost."

As I forestated, there's a difference between a bed and a coffin. The bed is for temporary dwellings while the coffin is the final place your physical body will lay. The coffin is not designed for the living, but for the dead. Nor is the bed designed for the dead, but for the living. When we speak about death, we are not speaking about it in a one-sided manner.

There are various types of death, but only one is permanent. A person can die, emotionally, physically and spiritually. A person can be breathing but have no compassion nor concern for anyone or anything. I've come across people that appeared to have no love and no feelings. That's what I consider emotional death. Then, there is physical death. The ultimate form of physical death is when the heart and all the organs in the body cease to function. But the body doesn't have to die all at once. There are times when parts of the body fail to operate even when other parts remain working. But eventually everything will stop. Then there's spiritual death. I consider that to be when a person has no acknowledgement of or relationship with God, or the true and living God.

Although there are differing aspects about life and death, they take on new meaning as a believer in the resurrection. Death to a nonbeliever and the unsaved is the end of life. But death to the believers in Christ Jesus is recognized as sleep. Often you can read in scripture the phrase "they slept with their fathers." I conclude that this is for the sole purpose of distinguishing the difference between life and death. When people sleep, they are expected to awaken. When people die, they are not expected to awaken. In the Gospel of John, chapter 11, Jesus refers to the death of Lazarus as sleep.

St. John 11:11-14 KJV

¹¹ Our friend Lazarus sleepeth; but I go, that I may awake him out of sleep.

¹² Then said his disciples, Lord, if he sleep, he shall do well.

¹³ Howbeit Jesus spake of his death: but they thought that he had spoken of taking of rest in sleep.

¹⁴ Then said Jesus unto them plainly, Lazarus is dead.

It was spoken of as sleep because sleep is a temporary state that all things that have breath do to rest. Those of us who are in the Lord that die in the Lord, will rise from death when we are called.

The only way death can be avoided in the physical body.

Although death is inevitable, there is a way that it can be avoided. But, there's only one way that physical death will not take place and it's only for the believers. This maneuver around death is only obtainable to those who accept the finished work of Jesus and by repenting from your sins. Upon Jesus' return, those who are still alive at that time who are in Christ will not see physical death. When you repent of your sins, a spiritual death takes place and you become alive in Christ Jesus in the spirit.

1 Corinthians 15:51-52 KJV

^{51}Behold, I shew you a mystery; We shall not all sleep, but we shall all be changed,

^{52}In a moment, in the twinkling of an eye, at the last trump: for the trumpet shall sound, and the dead shall be raised incorruptible, and we shall be changed.

My Conclusion:

In my conclusion, I once again want to interject a portion of the Admiral's speech.

"Making your bed will reinforce the fact that the little things in life matter. If you can't do the little things right, you'll never be able to do the big things right."

It is my hope and expectation that this act of making up your bed will be viewed in a way that will continue to remind us that each day is a blessing. Plus, all tasks have value and importance and we have an opportunity and responsibility to fulfill to the best of our ability the tasks ascribed to each and every one of us. Do what you can while you can. So that when you are no longer able to do as you once were, you can look back over your life and echo the words of the apostle Paul.

2 Timothy 4:7 KJV

"I have fought a good fight, I have finished my course, I have kept the faith:"

Therefore, live your life that God may be glorified and that you will be rewarded at the end of your life with eternal life. So, when the bed of sleep becomes your bed of transition and you are laid in your final resting place, you will be able to know that you will rise again in glory. When you receive the gift of love from God our father, who is Jesus the Christ, and you receive Him as your Lord and Savior, the grave becomes an entry door to everlasting life with Him. You will get up again. Amen

Romans 13: 11-14 NKJV

[11] And do this, knowing the time, that now it is high time to awake out of sleep; for now, our salvation is nearer than when we first believed.

¹² The night is far spent; the day is at hand. Therefore, let us cast off the works of darkness, and let us put on the armor of light.
¹³ Let us walk properly, as in the day, not in revelry and drunkenness, not in lewdness and lust, not in strife and envy.
¹⁴ But put on the Lord Jesus Christ, and make no provision for the flesh, to fulfill its lusts.

So, if you were blessed to wake up and the Lord gave you the strength to get up, then, get up, make your bed up, and do what you can, while you can. So, when you come to your final bed, you can arise to the call of your name and hear these words from the Father of all.

<u>Matthew: 25:23 KJV</u>
His lord said unto him, Well done, good and faithful servant; thou hast been faithful over a few things, I will make thee ruler over many

THE SIGNIFICANCE OF MAKING UP YOUR BED

things: enter thou into the joy of thy lord.
AMEN

AD Ministries

Pastor Alfred A. Dingle Sr.

About the Author

Alfred Alonzo Dingle is the fourth (4) child of six (6) children was born to Simon and the Late Vera (Davenport) Dingle. He is the father of three children, stepfather of three, and the grandfather of seven and is affectionately known to many young people as "POP." The Lord has gifted him to be a preacher, singer, writer and composer, musician, author, and with other talents. His musical gift has opened the doors and allowed him to play and sing at many churches and for many people and groups. In 2001, he recorded his first solo album entitled **"JESUS CARES,"** in which he wrote eight of the ten songs and re-arranged two. In 2002 he recorded his second, **"JUST A CLOSER WALK WITH THEE"** of which he re-arranged three songs and wrote one, also singing all the voices and playing all the instruments, except for the drums on some songs. In 2012, he recorded his third solo project, **"EMERGING FOR HIS GLORY,"** with all original songs written by him and doing more of the vocals and instruments. The Lord has blessed and is continuing to bless his preaching ministry. More and more doors are opening for him to do the work for the Kingdom of God. He has attended the

ABOUT THE AUTHOR

Baptist Brotherhood Bible Institute, T.H. Rankins Theological Clinic Bible Institute, and completed a host of other classes. He has been the pastor of the Memorial Baptist Church since July of 1996. He was a former member of Stellar Award nominated and Texas Gospel Music Award Group of the year, Singing Pastors of Piscataway, NJ for over five years. He has also written plays and many songs. He is the author of the book, **"The Church Held Hostage - The Plight of the Small Local Church"** and the book **"TRUE HINDRANCES – Misplaced Blame for Your Hindrances - Facing What's Really Stopping You From Pursuing Your Dreams"** which are available now. In addition, he is a former recording artist with the Janayra Music group of Georgia and currently has a single "Had It Not Been for Jesus" available through CD baby from the album "Emerging for His Glory," which is also available. He is a three-time McDonald's Gospelfest finalist for 2016 to 2018.

He is a member of the Historic Newark Symphony Hall Ministers' Council led by Dr. Albert J. Lewis, who serves as curator under Mr. Denmark. He was honored in June of 2017 by the City of Newark, and the state council for his work in the city. In December of 2016, he was blessed to minister in music for the Honoring of Three Mayors given by Mayor Ras. J. Baraka. Honored were past mayors of Newark, NJ, Sharp James and Kenneth Allen Gibson. Just to name a couple. He is currently a member of the 2015 McDonald Gospelfest winning group, **4 For Christ**. But most of all, he is a child of the Almighty God and a preacher of the Gospel of Jesus Christ.

ORDER INFORMATION

You can order additional copies of The Significance of Making Up Your Bed by emailing the author directly using the email address below.

Rev. Alfred A. Dingle Sr.

Email Address: revaldingle@yahoo.com

Books are available at Amazon.com,
Kindle and Your Local Bookstores (By Request)

Please leave a review for this book on Amazon and let other readers know how much you enjoyed reading it.

Thank you!

www.ingramcontent.com/pod-product-compliance
Lightning Source LLC
Chambersburg PA
CBHW062000070426
42450CB00025BA/1510